The Original
Road Kill Cookbook

The Original
Road Kill Cookbook

By B. R. "Buck" Peterson

Illustrations by "Sourdough" J. Angus McLean

Ten Speed Press

Official disclaimer: Buck assumes no responsibility for any of the information, techniques or suggestions in this very important survival guide. While he knows the absolute necessity of putting this backwoods bible in the hands of the hungry, Buck is a law-abiding, God-fearing sportsman, and a man for all seasons. Ditto on the responsibility for Ten Speed Press.

1☺ TEN SPEED PRESS
P.O. Box 7123
Berkeley, California 94707

Cover design by Brent Beck
Type set by Haru Composition

Library of Congress Cataloging-in-Publication Data

Peterson, B. R.
    The original road kill cookbook.

    1. Cookery—Anecdotes, facetiae, satire, etc.
I. Title.
PN6231.C624P4   1987   818'.5402   86-30178
ISBN 0-89815-200-3

Printed in the United States of America

    3 4 5 — 91 90 89 88

To: Mark "Boom Boom" Michalewicz, roadside chef extraordinaire, scourge of northwestern Alaska and often seen along the Yukon River and the back bays of Amber Lake with bare-breasted natives—for his survival preparation of domestic meats.

To: Robert "Roulette" Morel, high-rolling rodeo rocket, Chevy driver, and alleged suspect in the now famous "California Cat Caper," collector of dried cat-tails—for his felicitous feline fillets recipes.

To: All those other renegades, Budweiser bums, Indian mystics, and track jockies who have shared their recipes, anecdotes, and ideas.

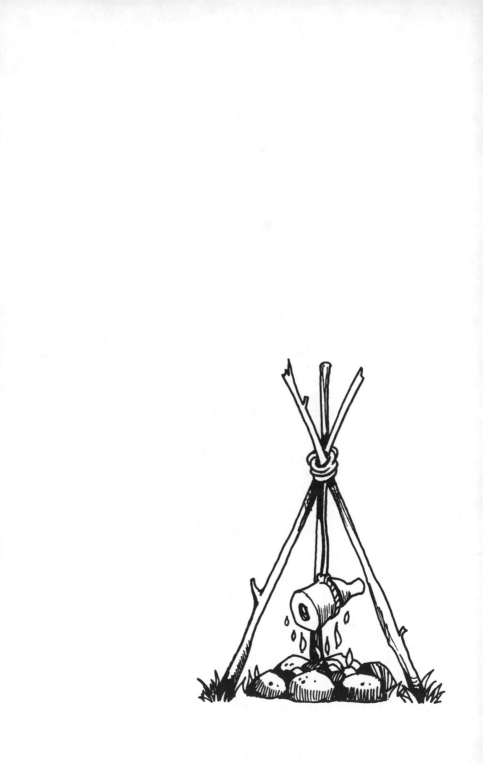

Contents

Foreword

Have you ever noticed how fat game wardens' kids are? You know — that marbley fat that comes from three squares a day? Can a lower level civil servant make that much money? We know that they are successful in their own hunts within their own hunting cabals, but still that won't fill the freezer on a regular basis. The key is in a letter from a Department of Fish & Game of a large western state: "Our yearly loss of big game from road kills is estimated to be 2,700 animals." This information is taken from reports by our *game warden!* "Although it is *unlawful* to pick up a road kill in our state, with our high unemployment rate, our wardens are finding that many road kills are disappearing before they can pick them up!"

Does it come together yet? Game wardens will typically say they snap up the large road kills to either give them to local charities (who probably don't like game meat) or study them for estimates on the health of the herd. Oh sure!

But now there is competition for the roadside rib-eye. It is, of course, in the aforementioned letter. The unemployed are being blamed for the illegal act of stealing chops from the warden's or patrolman's dinner table.

The *Original Road Kill Cookbook* is for the roadside shopper, that free-spirited American who wants to participate in Mother Nature's bounty. It's designed for both the motorist who purchased the critter with his own shopping cart and the casual shopper who stumbled onto good fortune either by accident or by design.

If you purchased a large animal with your own vehicle, you have possibly made a costly visit to the highway supermarket. Insurance companies report that the average deer-car encounter ends up costing at least $350. If you carry comprehensive insurance, you're only out the deductible. Charge it against at least 50 pounds of fresh deer meat, equal in quality to beef costing $2 a pound.

If you can utilize your day and energies to take advantage of other's shopping prowess, you are indeed fortunate! No damage, no guilt—the only thing you need is a good eye for a blood spore and then the ability to judge what's saveable. You'll spend lonely hours cruising likely areas for a fresh item. Generally, if it's cold out and the kill is fresh, the prime cuts are usually yours! Heat is your enemy —direct sunlight and high temperatures both work against the roadside shopper. If the skinned flesh isn't moist, firm yet with some texture, pass it by! The market is still open up the road!

This recipe book is meant to be easy to read and use. There are others you can buy; for example, if you want the recipe for pheasant lock a leekie, buy the L. L. Bean Game and Fish Cookbook. It's really best to just pick up a general cookbook and cook off critters as you would anything else. You know, you might just do as well cooking birds as you cook fish! Really, what difference does it make, it's just food.

Shopping will get better. Experts estimate that car-deer accidents will increase at a rate of 10% annually. When you are working with high base figures, such as the annual harvest of 12,000 deer in Minnesota alone (and that's only the reported incidents), you can appreciate what a supermarket exists out there!

Shopping is getting easier, too. The highest percentages occur near large metropolitan centers. Suburban Minneapolis-St. Paul is the most likely place to purchase a deer in Minnesota as is the greater Anchorage area for Alaska moose.

Remember, game meats can be used in all your traditional recipes, with the possible exception of those that don't already have them, like tapioca pudding.

the ROADSIDE SHOPPER

How to Shop
Yellowline Yummies

It's very important to purchase only the freshest meats for your dinner table. There are several ways to do this.

You may use your own shopping cart to dispatch your furred or feathered kindred souls to the celestial wild kingdom.

With the presence of mind of a smart shopper in those last split seconds before their bells toll, aim for the least preferred goods; on a large animal, start at the head and work backwards.

On a head shot, it'll just be a slap against the grill or corner of the windshield. Buck was on the rider side when a horse was hit and its head just popped the corner of the safety glass. The car was still kept under control, however, and this is important.

On a body shot, the large animal will either go under you (see Highway Hash), through your windshield (unlikely), or over the top (handy if you have an open bed pick-up).

On small animals, give them a shot in the head (except a dog, which is, on an open fire, a four-legged skin-on Dutch oven!).

On birds, it doesn't make any difference since they seldom hit straight on and their wings will protect their delicate breasts.

If you have to rely on the antics and disguised misfortunes of just the road clumsy, cruise the area most likely to produce close encounters of the collision kind. If your rig is equipped with a CB, tune it to the highway patrol and/or game warden frequency and your odds are good to beat those uniforms sitting mindlessly at the local Dunkin Donut. The bold might even approach the local

enforcement folks with ticket stubs to the policemen's ball sticking prominently out of pocket, and volunteer to remove unwanted carcasses from the highways.

Buck prefers to drive a made-in-America car, one of those road cruisers, late 50's, early 60's with the real big chrome bumpers. Second choice is a Ford Ranger, but the problem with pick-ups is that they often sit too high off the ground for small game purchases. They do have nice trunks though, and can go four-wheeling if a chase is on. Third choice is a real old European sedan, not from the south where Latins chase senoritas up boulevards but the Mercedes and Volvos—cars that have the weight, large deep trunks and general disrepair that roadside shoppers seem to prefer. Last choice are the imitation autos from the Orient —tin buckets powered by washing machine motors that are dangerous for both driver and his roadside intentions.

Don't forget the potential of bicycles, tricycles, wagons, wheelchairs and skateboards in pavement pursuits. With these, however, you might want to restrict your aim to small game.

Special note on equipment: It's handy to have a good, deep tire tread as it marks the meat like a good grill. It's *really* handy to have tire studs as they tenderize nicely.

When to Shop

As experienced game wardens know, it's best during the rut, October and November, when large animals' interests turn to romance.

When the food supply changes; first frost and then snow.

During the fawning season, typically May; when the original families are broken up by the arrival of the stork.

When there are interruptions in migrations, such as:

Where to Shop

"Badges" in their blue and whites know best in the rush to the roadside rib-eyes. Their four favorites are

NEAR:

WATER

GAME REFUGE

HEAVY COVER

DEER CROSSING

Equipment List

COOKBOOK

KNIFE

ONION

SALT & PEPPER

MATCHES

Buck also requires a half-rack of long-neck Buds on his list, one to start the day of shopping and a second or third to celebrate the pickings.

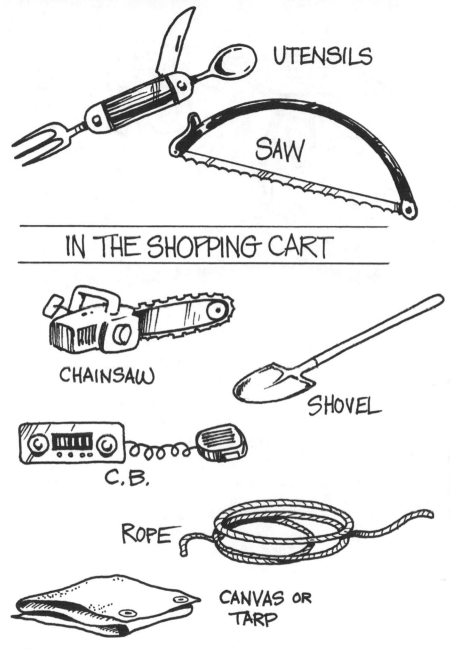

UTENSILS

SAW

IN THE SHOPPING CART

CHAINSAW

SHOVEL

C.B.

ROPE

CANVAS or TARP

There are other less obvious necessities—like enough gas to get you quickly home. Once loaded, don't speed and give the "badges" a second chance on your booty.

BIG GAME

"Oh, give me a road, where the buffalo roam, where the deer and the antelope play . . ."

Reports on successful shopping for large game come from all over the good ol' U.S. of A. It's estimated that over 150,000 deer alone are dispatched each year in deer-vehicle collisions. The highest losses come from those states with good roads, lotsa folks, and high game populations, like New York and Pennsylvania.

They bite the dust everywhere. Over 500 moose are run over in Alaska alone and most of these were near town. North Carolina reports an annual harvest of over 30 black bear. Wyoming calls in with a minimum of 1,000 antelope a year. Even the northeast region of Colorado typically produces at least one bighorn sheep a year!

Figures for the domestic darlings like the horse and cow are more difficult to gather. Whatever, when you purchase any of the large animals, you are making an investment in time and energy, if not auto equipment.

If you've hit a horse or cow in an open range state, you've made the majors! Good ol' boys with pointy boots and lantern jaws don't cotton to herd reduction by strangers and you may need your checkbook. If it's dark out and the carcass is almost out of sight from traffic, with a little push you *two* are on a roll!

If someone before you didn't pick up their special, it's very important to estimate the bounty. If the flesh feels warm and soft, you may be in luck; start your analysis and look for the best cuts. If the flesh feels warm and hard, you're in a warm climate and out of luck . . . keep shopping.

Roadside Preliminaries

If you purchased the animal with your own vehicle, moral outrage is usually enough for you to throw the beast in your trunk and speed away to safer grounds. Some states require disposal permits, some say you can't have it anyway, and some don't care. Make an anonymous call to the Fish & Game Department before your first shopping trip.

With a large purchase, you have three choices, each with factors of time and condition of animal.

First and foremost, you'll want to take the meat that's good to eat—particularly that which did not have direct contact with your bumper or become tainted by ruptured rumens (stomachs).

If you are a good sport and the purchase is new, take it all, guided by the following dictums:

    A. Field dress it as soon as possible (see Buck's Butcher Shop).
    B. Skin it, taking the hide off like you would an overcoat.
    C. Save the camp meats.

If My Friend Flicka has just crossed the final finish line, be assured that thoroughbreds taste as good as a Carni-Shetland. Their owners are usually drinking buddies with circuit judges, so caution is critical here.

If you are in a hurry, at least take the meat that's good:

A. Crank up your chainsaw and quarter out the good vittles.
B. Bury the rest.

If you have a lot of time and the meat is good:

A. Drag carcass to a hidden spot and gut.
B. Butcher carcass, removing all large portions without bones (see Buck's Butcher Shop).
C. Bury the rest. Treat yourself to a Michelin meal!

Bear

The flesh of the bear, a vegetarian with an occasional taste for University of Utah bear experts, is a special treat, especially from a young bruin. Man has tried to taint their natural flavor by placing garbage dumps near their traditional feeding areas, but generally a bear will taste good and if you're able to shop near a national park like Yellowstone, they may even contain a hint of Twinkies and Frito-Lay bean dip.

If you've hit a polar bear, don't eat the liver—too much vitamin A. After butchering, remove all excess fat and cook it according to cut; roast, chops, etc. Like pork, cook until well done to eliminate dangers of trichinosis. Buck's family enjoys the roast in particular.

Roast Smokey

Soak roast overnight in water with vinegar.
Wash roast, dry and season with salt and pepper.
Lard the meat with either bacon or salt pork.
Roast at 325° for 40 minutes per pound.
With red wine covering bottom of pan, baste occasionally.

Elk

This large member of the deer family is found in the high mountain country of the West and is second only to the moose in roadside bargains. As in all red meat recipes, elk can be a perfect substitute for beef. *Caution:* The elk is considered an important game animal in the western states, particularly to the few remaining underfed game wardens.

Make sure you purchase your critter quickly and quietly. Don't forget to pull the buck molars as they are ivory and can make nice ornamental jewelry. If you've bought an antlered animal, save the rack to sell to oriental people who grind them up for aphrodisiacs, or if you think there's already too many oriental people, hang them in your basement.

Elk seem to end up as steaks, chops, roasts, and the rest thrown into hamburger or sausage. Buck likes to marinate his steaks with tabasco juice, burgundy, a little lemon juice, and lots of pepper overnight and then in an alcohol-induced cooking frenzy, flash-fry, or sear the fillets in hot butter and serve rare.

Deer

If you can't be a deerslayer, you should have your keys taken from you! With their habit of stopping and staring at headlights, all you have to do is aim your motorized missile towards their lunch bucket and bingo, Bambi bites the dust! If you're leary to use your own cart, mosey down roads used by large trucks. The big tractor-trailers don't even slow down as they crash through deer playing tar tag. With a full larder of venison, you can comfortably sit out a winter waiting for the job offer you deserve.

Buck debones all his venison and pan-fries the steak and chops! Remove all the fat, soak in your favorite marinade overnight (if you have an old buck), and fry the steaks in the same pan you made homefries in. The camp meats, especially the liver, are particularly good, especially sliced thin, rolled in flour and again pan-fried, covered with onions. If you can't wait till you get home, cut the slices an inch or more thick and grill over an open fire—just enough to crisp the outside!

Antelope

Shoppers in states like Wyoming often find this prairie goat on special. Some may have found the meat a bit strong, but that usually comes from improper cooking or field handling. A hunter pal from Wyoming, as wiry as the flatland goat himself, always skins the animal immediately upon purchase, taking great care to keep the hair from touching the flesh. This removal cools the meat too.

Buck likes the backstrap best, that long filet that runs along the backbone, and the best way to eat those is to cut into 1 inch mignons and flash-fried in butter in a hot pan. A good way to cook the larger steaks is:

Saute onion slices in oil and butter.
Sear steaks separately on both sides.
Add onions, water, cover and simmer for 15-20 minutes.
Add one can mushroom soup—cover and simmer until tender.

Moose

Bullwinkle has an attention span problem. It's figured that it takes eleven seconds for an image to register in the peabrain of this rangy recluse. In that short time, you can punch his ticket to meet St. Peter! The four-legged meat counters are as high-strung as an old woman, and with their skinny legs and bulky torso, look like one too. Luckily, they don't taste like one—pound for pound, properly prepared moose meat cannot be matched. The sheer size slows a few shoppers, but a sharp chainsaw can reduce your problems: First gut and then quarter the best for a speedy trip home. *Caution:* Moose are highly prized game animals, so don't dally! Moose is a major purchase, so cut out a saddle (see Buck's Butcher Shop) and invite your drinking buddies over.

Rub saddle with butter and a little cut garlic.
Put in pre-heated oven, on rack, uncovered and cook at 350° to your preference.
Make your own gravy and serve over wild rice.

P.S. In heavy snows, moose show up along and on old railroad tracks and are properly considered fair game for the rail-roadside shopper!

Cow

Rustling is defined in some western states as an unhealthy activity involving desperados snatching Elsie from the ranchers' free government grazelands and selling her for profit to filet fences in the dark of night. Surely an animal brought to an early demise as the result of an unavoidable accident is not grounds for civil action or uncivil roadside response. Remember, in any American court (except Wyoming, Nebraska, Montana, Texas, or any other beef state), you are innocent until proven guilty on this one.

It's important to be a good neighbor and responsible citizen. To leave a large animal on the road, roadside, or let's even go further, within driving distance from the road's edge, is irresponsible and morally wrong. Winch that animal into the back of your pickup, throw the tarp over it and let your conscience be your guide. Remember your hungry youngins!

Recipes? You're asking *Buck* for recipes for corn-fed beef?

Horse

When the black stallion lies down for a nap and dreams of his Hollywood sequel, you'd easily mistake it for dead. Poke it with a stick before you start taking out the tenderloins!

Horse meat has shown up frequently throughout history as a foodstuff—during the siege of Paris, Napoleon's march into Russia, on Donner Pass, and in fashionable homes in the northern Rockies. Japanese people eat horse meat as sashimi. Dress out this noble beast of burden as any large animal and use your favorite red meat recipe, including ours:

Tournedos of Trigger

Ingredients: Trigger steak cut from loin, cracked pepper, fresh thyme, red wine, broken horsebones, onions, celery, carrots, wild sprouts, bacon.

Wrap trigger steak in bacon and fasten with toothpick, season with pepper.
Sear tournedos in hot skillet until brown on both sides. Remove from pan.
Add vegetables and seasoning. Cook for 5 minutes, stirring constantly. Add red wine, reduce by half, add horse sauce. Simmer for 15 minutes, strain.
Serve tournedos with sauce, garnish with horse bone marrow, and serve hoof to accompany.

Happy Trails!

SMALL GAME

Taking a large animal may seem like a lot of work, so many galloping gourmets shop for their small cousins. Your odds certainly are better! Thousands, maybe millions of cartoon characters enter the celestial magic kingdom every year. There's more variety, the marketplace more convenient, and the damages to your go-cart is always less — unless you're a motorized Mr. McGregor torquing up a sandbank after Flopsy and Mopsy.

The preparations described are for a small sampling of Mother Nature's little people. Road kill reports from these great 50 states also include fox, bobcat, mink, armadillos, and sasquatches.

Never mind, all of the recipes will at least work. The principal caution here is the incidence of rabies in several species such as skunk. If an animal looks or smells rabid, do not eat or touch with your tongue or once touched with your fingers, insert them along the inner sensitive tissues of your nose.

Windshield Wabbit

Young bucks, such as Thumper, need only a couple hours of soaking in salt water to draw off blood, but old Bugs should be soaked up to 18 hours to draw out the orneriness!

To clean wabbit, cut stomach from butt to ribs, hold by the front legs and snap quickly; the guts will just fly out, usually all over your partner's gear if not careful.

Barbecued Bugs Bunny

Cut rabbit into serving pieces.
Put on rack in baking pan.
Bake 1¼ hours in hot oven.
Brush every 15 minutes with barbecue sauce.

BONUS SECTION

Most of the furry friends have skin coverings that would look equally as good on your head, around your old lady's neck, or pieced together, as a second, more attractive skin for you or your loved ones. Use caution and a sharp knife as you remove the garment! Salt the inside and stretch on a board until the hide becomes dry and workable. To fashion a hat, especially if you have the time, tie the hide on your head and let dry pre-formed.

A cleaner way to do this is to take the hide to a good tanner and then let a leather crafter create a new fashion for you!

Squirrel
Treetop Tidbits

These little guys are Buck's favorite small game. They act like little people with their own culture and once undressed, even look like little people. You've noticed how often they are in cartoons and used to describe people like your neighbors. Well, those little speeders turn on a chestnut and are hard to shop for. If you're quick, you'll find the meat mild in flavor, fine textured, and delicious! A sure-fire way to cook nature's squirrelies:

Stew

Cut up carcass into 4 pieces.
Brown pieces in margarine or butter.
Cover with water, season very lightly.
Simmer until almost done.
Add diced, sliced, shredded favorite vegetables.
Mix ½ cup water and 6 tablespoons flour and thicken brew.
Now cook until done.

BONUS SECTION

Sheldon's, a fishing lure manufacturer in Antigo, Wisconsin, buys good quality squirrel tails, so send off for their instructions (626 Center St., Antigo, WI 54409-2496).

Raccoon

Buck met his first garbage can dweller emptying 55-gallon drums of tourist trash in a county park in northern Michigan. It proved to be a feast of no small proportions—it's flat out delicious when roasted. Make sure you get those scent glands off from under the front legs and thighs. The famous recipe is:

Roast Rocky Raccoon

Cook the clean carcass in the oven for about 3 hours in a slow oven (300°).
Baste frequently with drippings every 30 minutes.
Make gravy from the drippings.
Season and serve with yams.

P.S. Many will stuff with their favorite flavored dressings.

Mother Nature's "Special" Animals

There are a number of God's creatures that have the misfortune of being ugly, smelly, greasy, dangerous, fish-eating, skin-covered garbage bags. Some of these are thought to be eaten only by members of inferior races and low economic classes. This is not just and this cookbook will put these tasty morsels within reach of all of us. The top seven contenders are the beaver, muskrat, opossum, porcupine, badger, wolverine, and skunk.

These animals may need special handling, both at the time of purchase and during preparation.

ROADSIDE

Many of these animals have stink glands, usually under their forelegs and along the small of their back. They must be removed. Remove all fat, cleaning the carcass carefully so no glands are ruptured on the good meat.

HOME

Many gourmets would soak a carcass overnight in salt water. Young animals won't need more than 8 hours in the tub, while old critters could stand a 24-hour soak. Some would add a cup of vinegar and a pinch of salt to each quart of water.

Beaver

This friendly vegetarian is prized by old trappers and reprobates. The small yearlings are so tender when cooked properly that all you'll need is a spoon. On Bucky Beaver, take care to remove all the fat and musk glands or castors just under the skin in front of the genitals. Soak the critter overnight and then cook it as you would a large bird. If, however, your furry friend had its castors and cajones unproperly stirred by a Toyota 4X4, you have just one good option left:

Beaver Tail

Skin the tail and wash it well.
Cover in a pot with water and a couple tablespoons of vinegar.
Cook until tender.
Drain and cut into slices like a London Broil.
Dip slices in beaten egg and roll in bread crumbs.
Fry until golden brown.

OR

Instead of cutting into slices, cut into chunks.
Add to 2 quarts of boiling water.
Add carrots, celery, onions and cook until vegetables are done.
Add egg noodles and drained peas.

OR

Add chunks to your favorite pea soup or baked beans.

P.S. I've never known anyone who has tried this.

Muskrat

If any animal was misnamed, this marsh mammal is—it does not deserve the rat suffix. It's a quiet little animal, living on grasses and vegetables of the marsh, hence its marsh rabbit nickname. Its dark meat is prized by old shoppers and Swedish people. In fact, not too long ago Minnesota Swedes ate as much muskrat as they did wolverine (the taking of the latter left a lot of Finlanders without a patron saint). The best ways to eat this critter is to roast, pan-fry, or stew.

BONUS SECTION

Skin this beast carefully as its fur is still valuable in the production of old coats that smell up your grandmother's cloakroom.

Pavement Possum

It's not true possums are born dead on the side of the road. They are a favorite of roadside shoppers in many parts of this wonderful country and most will take the whole animal home for cooking as they are delicious stuffed. Old timers will age this sweetness a couple days. They are good broiled over a campfire or fried along the railroad tracks! Good ol' boys will often just scald, scrape, and roast the beast like a hog—traditional accompaniment is persimmons.

Roast Possum

Stuff the carcass with your favorite bread dressing.
Salt and pepper to taste, inside and out.
Bake in an uncovered pan for 2 to 2½ hours, basting frequently with butter and sprinkling a little brown sugar. Skim grease as it accumulates.
45 minutes before taking the possum out, ring the carcass with canned sweet potatoes or parboiled sweet yams and sprinkle again with brown sugar. Bake until crusty.

Porcupine

On a trip to the northwoods one weekend to set up deer stands, we purchased two plump porkies and after gutting them, brought them home to feed our hungry brothers and sisters. Skinning the first animal, we found this vegetarian ready for the winter with a carcass surrounded by marbly, greasy fat; yet once cleaned, provided fine dining. The second of God's little creatures was given to the local minister unclean (since Buck didn't want to clean another greasy gut-bag!) and there was never another inquiry about our hunting trips. *Tip:* Make a mulligan stew or at least a pate from their oversized livers.

You can skin the quill pig by starting on the stomach where there are no quills. Gut, clean, and then roast the carcass, or the preferred and whole parts such as the hind legs.

Badger, Wolverine, Woodchuck

You hardly ever see the first two unless you're trailbiking in their backyards. The badger has a nice pair of back legs, while the wolverine is so damn ornery, it might just bite you back. The woodchuck is a varmint about the same size so treat all three alike.

Chop off head and feet.
Skin by cutting into skin, back or belly and pull over carcass.
Gut, clean, and disjoint.
Brown pieces in a little margarine and season.
Cover with water, simmer for several hours.
Add your favorite vegetables just before meat is done.

Dog

As in all meat preparations, the quality of the meat will influence the recipe. Dog meat is considered a delicacy by Polynesians, Chinese, and a few Europeans. Brigit Bardot says "Eating dog . . . is a horror in itself," but what does that old frog actress know? The sleek tire-biters can be stringy and tough, while just-weaned pups should be tender vittles. Buck's grandmother's favorites are:

Hushed Puppies

Two small dogs cut up into small chunks.
Add potatoes, carrots, cabbage, onions, and celery.
Put all ingredients in a large pot with a quart or so of water and bring to a boil.
Lower heat, cover, and cook until done.

(Clean it up since there is no one left to throw the scraps to!)

Poached Pooch

This works for those old hound dogs that twitch when they sleep.

Heat to boiling a quart of water, some salt, and a little lemon juice in a large skillet.
Add sliced loins of Lassie.
Simmer slowly until done.

Just remember, those village princesses and war lords of Polynesia have treasured Pluto Paté since the beginning of my memory. Do you remember seeing pets in *Mutiny on the Bounty*? Those bronzed aborigines, probably with anthropologists standing idly by, fill sacks with likely candidates and prepare the meat like Mexicans swatting pinatas — with clubs! The Garden of Eden reveals its mysteries slowly! Do not let sleeping dogs lie — roust them with your roadster!

Skunk

This decorative pet is very good french fried, and its pelt makes a great looking hat.

Make sure Fifi is in skunk heaven before skinning.
Carefully remove all the musk glands, in particular, those two grape-sized glands at the base of the tail. If you push too hard, sweet scents will waft your way and you'll bathe in tomato juice that night.

Cut animal into chunks.
Parboil the chunks until tender (about an hour).
Occasionally remove scum off top.
Remove meat.
Make thick batter of egg yolks, flour, milk, and salt.
Deep fry in fat at 360° until golden brown.

Curbside Cat

A roadside shopper has to move fast on these as cat owners miss their tabby all too quickly and will want to bury them in some fancy pet cemetery with all their limbs intact. If you're quick with a blade, it's really clever to skin "snookums" on the spot and leave its outer garment close by, causing Miss Marple to think her baby has just been scared out of her ninth life and will soon return to share the next bowl of fishheads.

Skin and clean Poopsie like you would a squirrel.
Stuff the cavity with dressing and tie front legs back and back legs forward.
Lay breast down in a low baking pan, uncovered, with bacon strips across back.
Roast at 325° for one hour, remove and make gravy from drippings.
As you dig in, recall all the midnight howling and torn garbage bags.

Curbside Cat
OPTION #2

Same recipe as above but put a two-pound catfish inside the cavity and drape anchovy strips over the carcass before roasting.

Serve on a single large leaf of lettuce lying in a hollow of non-scented cat litter on a wide platter.

Tell Miss Marple dinner is ready.

Asphalt Armadillo
(On the Half Shell)

Two thousand pounds of Detroit steel will prepare this armored throwback for your youngins! You'll want a very fresh purchase here as heat, dirt or just stink sets in and it'll soon be fit only for your mother-in-law.

Instructions: If the underside isn't bumper split, do so and clean out all the stuff you won't eat (the innards). Cut the little rascal out of the shell. Once out of its protective cover, you can cook this critter off in very traditional ways. Buck likes to bake it with stuffing! It would be really clever of you to stuff it with what a live one eats—roots, angle-worms, one garden variety vegetable and a few ground bugs for color. Others might just cut up and pan-fry them like chicken, or you might just want to experiment. After cooking, make a paste or puree in your food processor—whatever, you'd be making a food statement even Mother Nature could be proud of!

Rodents

Far too little has been said regarding the food value of our little furry friends. Small field mice in a stew cooked over an open fire can, at the very least, provide a hot meal and the tails are handy for cocktail dipping.

Mouse Mulligan

Skin, gut, and boil first, then simmer animals until tender.
Include livers as they are high in protein.
Add carrots, potatoes, onions, salt, pepper, tomatoes, and bacon bits.
Cook until vegetables are tender. Add flour and water to thicken and cook 10 to 15 minutes more.

If your catch has just crawled off a boat of foreign registry, caution is advised, but if you boil the hell out of the carcass first, you can move on to:

Rat Ragout

Ingredients: Rodent, onions, celery, carrots, wild mushrooms, juniper berries, Wild Turkey, mouse sauce, oil.

Marinate skinned tenderized rat in juniper berries, Wild Turkey, thyme, onions, celery, and carrots for 8 hours. Drain, pat dry, sear disjointed rat in hot oil in skillet, add marinade and simmer until reduced by half.
Add mouse sauce and simmer for 20 minutes.
Serve with orzo pasta and cheese bread.

Frog

On nights of high electric storm activity in the Midwest, frogs would leave their lily pads and head for the bright lights of town. They would grease a highway, yet most people would be content to drive right on by this food display. Their appendages are rare delicacies, both front and hind legs, and are particularly fine for a roadside snack before a drive-in movie and some "pining" with your favorite lady.

Legs

Take the smaller frogs for their sweeter, more tender legs.
Strip the skin as you would take off a glove.
Grill over an open flame.

OR

At home, roll in lightly salted and peppered flour or bread crumbs.
Fry in butter over low heat until meat falls off from bones.

OR

Fry in hot deep fat a few minutes until brown.

Over 200 million pairs of legs are consumed in fine eateries in the West—now bring this fine dining home.

Wa Wa Ron
(Bull Frog)

Cajun French musician V. Fontenot times his shopping carefully so they beat themselves senseless jumping up and down. If your timing is off, all you'll get is a greenish oil patch on the road. When cleaning, cut tendons or your crepes will jump off the table. Fry Wa Wa Ron legs as you would chicken. Make crepes using your favorite pancake recipe. Take deboned fried legs and roll up in crepes. Serve with Jimmy Newman's homemade pepper jelly.

BUCK'S SPECIAL SHOPPING TIP...

" I like to shop on unlit local roadways after dark: best time is the two hours after Sunset, especially on daylight saving time."

Snake

A snake should be approached with caution. May the first bite be yours!

Cut a circle through skin behind head and pull hide back towards tail.
Remove head and tail.
Remove entrails and wash thoroughly.
Roast on a stick.

P.S. Do not eat sea snakes.

Turtle

There was a small dark tavern in central Minnesota called the Dew Drop Inn that used to serve turtle, all you could eat for a couple bucks on Fridays only. With a couple beers, a turtle feast is a great way to start a weekend. Don't fool around with "pet" turtles, shop for a snapper!

If still alive, have it bite on a stick and behead with an axe.
Put turtle in boiling water for 5 to 8 minutes — it relaxes the muscles.
Cut off claws and, turned over, cut skin all way around.
Pull skin down legs to feet and cut off feet.
With a sharp knife or saw, cut substance connecting top and bottom shells and pry off bottom.
Remove entrails and all yellow fat.
Cut out four quarters and soak overnight in salt water.

Brown meat in margarine or fat in frying pan.
Add several onions and cover with water to simmer until tender.
Put in mashed potatoes, cover with gravy made from pan juices and flour and enjoy!

OR

Salt and pepper the meat like beef and fry to your taste.

Lizard, Newt, Salamander

There is a reason and purpose for every animal. One is to be a link in the food chain leading up to us higher beings. Climbing down from this lofty view of these hideous creatures, Buck recommends that during cleaning, eat crackers so you don't blow your previous meal.

Remove the head and skin. Boil, broil, or fry the meat.

Gator

Throw the critter on coals to loosen the plates.
Skin this prehistoric throwback.
A 10-foot gator will offer up 100 pounds of meat and it's fixed many ways—particularly good deep fried. You can fry the fingers as you would a bear paw or make any variation of meatballs, meatloaf, or a real favorite:

Gator Goulash

Ingredients: Gator stock, diced gator, paprika, onions, bay leaf, thyme, carrots, celery, new potatoes, flour, and fat.

In hot skillet, sear cubed gator with fat, season with salt, pepper, paprika, thyme, bay leaf, and vegetables.
Add flour, cook for 10 minutes.
Add gator stock, stir until thickened and smooth.
Simmer for 45 to 60 minutes or until gator is tender.
Serve piping hot with sourdough bread.

WATERFOWL

If you hit a whistler swan on the road bordering the game preserve or a big gander near the hobby farm, pull alongside the poor baby with your shopping cart, open the door quickly, pull it up and under your legs for a controlled getaway. If it's a pet, it is best the owners don't know—the kids will think their Donald Duck has flown south to Capistrano or wherever they go.

Find convenient water; a river or lake where you can gut the feathery friend and wash up the bird and yourself at the same time.

Decide then whether you'd prefer a roadside snack or fly home to your own nest. If you came to the supermarket hungry, take your penknife and cut just under the skin from gut to the neck and take out the two breasts. Roast these morsels over an open fire. It's easy to tell when the cooking's done: when pricked, the juices are no longer red and when the leg is cut from the body, the meat is no longer pink.

If you're heading home to a hungry family, field dress your birds as soon as possible. Put the livers in a sandwich bag for later use. Don't pluck yet! Wait till you are home to scald the bird in boiling water. This loosens the feathers. Another popular way to remove feathers is to dip the birds in hot paraffin or wax.

Datsun Duck

There is no duck you can't eat, even those you know have been doing slime shooters on the bottom of the marsh. Skin even the ugliest of them, clean well, stuff full of onions, and bake in a slow oven for a couple hours. Take onions out, replace with a favorite breaded dressing, and cook until tender.

Your chances of hitting diver ducks are few unless you are four-wheel driving through local swamps sucking down some local brew. You are more likely to come upon a sight Buck had several months ago of a hen mallard and eight ducklings walking across a busy road to a larger puddle. Cars carefully let them cross — a foolish gesture, as the presentation of a large mallard surrounded by eight smaller birdettes would win food critics' awards.

Two of Buck's favorite recipes:

Coot Cutlets

Remove breasts from as many birds as you've purchased. Put in your pocket and go home.
Soak in a beer bath for several days in the cooler.

Mix a couple eggs, salt, pepper, and dip breasts in mixture. Roll in bread crumbs.

Saute in hot oil until brown.
Lower heat and cover for a few more minutes.
Serve on a bed of rice, garnished with green and yellow vegetables.

Some like to put an onion inside the cavity of a fisheater, cover and keep overnight in a cool place before cooking.

Duck a la Orange

Make a stuffing of bread cubes, diced celery, and oranges.
Prepare Daffy Duck for his final roost by salting the clean cavity.
Stuff with good stuff listed above and cook in slow oven.
Baste with own juices every so often.
Just before done, swab orange marmalade on breast.
This will fulfill minimum wilderness requirement for vitamin C.

Gravel Goose

What's good for the gander, especially those honkers spitting at you in the county park, is a slap by your car grillwork. A wild goose chase will add a centerpiece to your Sunday buffet. It really doesn't matter which one you take. The old timers need a little extra care using moist heat, but it's worth the effort to put it to them.

Old Bird

Put a little margarine in the bottom of your Dutch oven and brown the entire bird, sealing in the essential juices.
Pick up a good cheap red wine and mix with a ratio of not more than 1/3 wine and 2/3 water.
Once all the sides are brown, cut the heat quickly and add water and wine to just below the halfway mark on the bird.
Slowly cook on low heat, *covered* until done.

Gravel Goose—*continued*

Young Bird

If you've bumped a yearling, bake it like a domestic bird.
Stuff with your favorite store-bought dressing.
Put in a roasting pan in a medium oven at 325°.
Cook until tender, usually 20 minutes per pound. Baste
often with natural juices.

Other Water Boids
Snipe, Whistler Swan, Flamingo, Etc.

You'd be surprised how many other exotic birds stroll
along the center line. It's important to lead them like you
would with a shotgun; judge which way they'll lift off and
coordinate a bumper kiss with the lowest part of their flight
pattern!

Stoke up the charcoal and barbecue these birds.
Rub butter, cut garlic on skin and then sprinkle paprika
over carcass.
Basting occasionally, cook over open coals until tender.

BASIL BONUS

Roadside shopper Vince takes a fancy to egrets feeding
alongside Louisiana roads, taking care to be properly
buckled up when swerve-shopping on the shoulder and
always taking a few extra as these white marsh birds are
real skinny.

Brown egret in iron pot, add onions, 1 clove garlic, 1 can
stewed tomatoes, 3 cups water.
Simmer till tender.
Add salt, pepper and basil to taste and serve on rice.

UPLAND BIRDS

Racing down a mountain road towards Irwin, Idaho one early fall morning, Buck leaned into a turn in the road and into a small covey of quail that had decided to see what was on the other side of the road. To his other passengers, the explosion of feathers and taps on the old grillwork were just more noises of a lengthy journey, and they didn't wake until Buck was halfway through cleaning the feathered darlings in a frosty mountain creek.

Upland game birds are particularly easy to shop for as they are plentiful and kinda stupid. Their small little bodies don't cause much harm to your mechanical monster and fit nicely in your pocket or glove compartment once cleaned.

There will always be some pipe-smoking, tweedy, pointy-headed armchair chef who'll argue the difference in taste between pheasant and partridge, grouse and chukkar. Some will even say the western variety tastes differently than their eastern cousins — Bullroar! Of course, diet will play a small part in their taste, but the quiche-eaters cover their birds' original taste in foreign-sounding sauces anyway. The only differences are the same that make you choose your women: size and age. A big old sage hen is tough, while a baby quail needs only to be warmed in your hands to be eaten. Once you get by the special preparations for these two variables, it's how you fix the bird that gets your taste buds cooking.

Most shoppers will fix their birds one of three ways: roasted, fried, or stewed. Stewing will take the orneriness out of the oldest sage grouse, frying is good for all sizes and pieces, and roasting is particularly good for those carcasses large enough to hold an onion. The only exception to any of the bird recipes is in fixing a vulture or buzzard. I'd recommend first boiling these butt-ugly scavengers at least ½ hour before cooking to kill any parasites.

Game Birds

Old birds should be cooked off with moist heat, and sometimes even that's not enough to soften up granddaddy's drumstick! If worse comes to worse, take the breast only and simmer over a low heat. The larger birds, like pheasant and partridge, are best easily roasted:

Stuff bird with your favorite dressing.
Place carcass in a medium oven (350° to 400°).
Cook off at least 20 minutes to a pound.

OR

Run a stick through the bird and bake over an open fire.

OR

If the bird is already disjointed having just been pulled off your radiator, cut into pieces and roll in flour. Brown the meat in hot fat or margarine and cook over low heat, adding a favorite wine for flavor.

Big Bird Special

Eboo (Owl) Gumbo. Shop at night, bring beer and have buddy spot owls swooping in front of your headlights. Bumper kiss them or speed up and let them fly into side of door.

Vince's gumbo calls for browning owl pieces in large iron pot, add chopped onions, 1 clove garlic, ½ pint prepared roux, salt and pepper.
Add sausage and 3 quarts water.
Simmer until tender and serve on rice.
Custom requires 1 more cup of water for each unexpected guest. Guess WHOOOS coming for dinner!

Tweety Birds

Sylvester the Cat had the right idea—tweety birds taste good, as do sparrows, bobolinks, and red-butted woodpeckers! The little breasts on a domestic darling swell to bite-size over their short life span and are superb roasted with a few bacon strips on top in a moderate oven for 45 minutes.

The bird road kill bonanza is becoming more rare—I mean the big starling swat by the jet of a 747! Cruel large airport operators are poisoning Mother Nature's babies with noxious drugs, but smaller airports such as the one in Jackson Hole, Wyoming are still good bets as the smallest jets ram through the matings of sage grouse.

The harbinger of spring, the robin, is a superb snack, and the basic recipe for all song birds is easy:

Remove breasts and wash well.
Dip in flour and brown only in butter.
Salt and pepper.
Remove and cook in pressure cooker for 10 minutes or so, or roadside, put on a grate over a pot of boiling water.
Enjoy as a main dish.

MISCELLANEOUS

Exotics

Buck learned from sources best left alone that there are body parts not described in any other part of this cookbook that have food value. These are items which are not manly to eat and you know which ones we're talking about. The others include:

HORN (antler): If on an early rut, out-of-season shopping trip, a buck deer in early velvet is carrying a hat of delicacies. Remove antler, scrape velvet off, cut into short lengths (2 to 3 inches), wash in salt water and bake until tender. Season and spread like jam on bread or biscuits.

BONE MARROW: Cut marrow bone into short pieces and freeze until use in stews. Or throw longer pieces into campfire, bake and break open for a late-night snack.

NOSES: Bulwinkles work well here. Cut off upper jaw just below the eyes and parboil for an hour. Cool and wash well. Put in a pot of fresh water with onions, salt, pepper, and simmer until tender. Cut the meat off into slices for Schnoz sandwiches.

EYES, EARS, HEAD: Some people will eat the muscle around the eyes. Buck won't. Ears on a roast pig are good. The head of a large animal you put on your wall.

Common Bags

STEW: The difference between stew and soup is the look of it, as far as Buck can tell. You put more stuff in stew; wine, broth, stock, and simmer it all longer.

KABOBS: Soak 1-inch cubes of any red meat in a marinade of burgundy wine, onion slices, and bacon bits for 5 to 6 hours. Put on a stick, alternate with vegetables (don't forget the onions!) and cook over hot coals, basting frequently until done. If you're doing birds, butter the outside, wrap in a cabbage leaf, and roast over an open fire as above.

JAMBALAYA: Cut meat in small portions. Heat oil in Dutch oven and fry celery, onions, green peppers, and tomatoes until soft. Add meat and brown. Cook meat over a very low heat for 30 minutes. Add a couple cups uncooked long grain rice, 1½ cups chicken broth, salt, pepper, cayenne pepper to taste, dash of powdered thyme and tabasco and cook slow till rice is done.

SOUP: Take a pound of wings, lips, ears, toes, or carcass of any game animal or bird. Add onions, carrots, celery and any other common vegetable, and cover with water. Simmer until meat is tender. Remove meat and cut into small pieces. Remove vegetables. Cook broth. Add noodles and cook off. Add meat and vegetables. Season.

Rocky Mountain Oysters
(Nuts To You!)

You'll want to take these off a real dead critter.

Cut the sack off and remove everything, including the thin membrane covering the cajones! Wash completely. Cut off both ends. Slice into bite-size pieces. Roll each in your favorite batter (suggestions: egg, then cracker crumbs or cornmeal). Fry in medium deep fat until golden brown.

P.S. You'll sing (soprano!) for more.

Vegetables

A neighbor's garden is the best place to shop for accompaniments. Watch their work schedule and habits of their pets. They will *never* use all of what they grow; in fact, if they know what you are doing, they'd probably thank you. Grocery stores will often discard the older veggie — you know, the browning lettuce that doesn't glisten under the high pressure water sprays — but you'll have to hurry now since food banks for never-do-wells are drying up this source of goods.

Use vegetables in quantities set by personal choice and availability. Buck recommends onions for everything. If you're roadside dining, make sure you gather your greens far enough away from any spraying road crew or vacationing pet.

Highway Hash

If you have the makings of a good hash, particularly if your studded 15-inch Uniroyals make a fresh delivery, make a meat hash. In fact, some shoppers will quickly strip and wash the edible meat, add a couple onions, potatoes, stalks of celery, throw all in an extra heavy Glad Bag and repeat the crime.

Pull the bag out from under your GMC, fry ingredients over low heat in bacon grease, season to taste and enjoy.

Camp Meat
How to Get Them

There are traditions in large hunting camps that special meats are prepared in celebration of major scores and good efforts. It's important, especially for new shoppers, that you know where the delicacies are and how to get them out, often in a hurry.

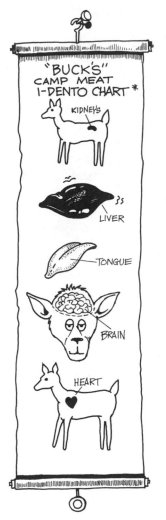

"BUCK'S" CAMP MEAT I-DENTO CHART *

KIDNEYS

LIVER

TONGUE

BRAIN

HEART

KIDNEYS: Cut through the skin just over where kidney punches are made.

LIVER: This large mass is, on large animals, a slippery, firm, dark red mass. It is loaded with protein. In small animals, especially the rabbit, inspect for infection. If you note anything suspicious like small white spots, throw all down a rat-hole, wash your hands, and keep shopping.

TONGUE: Slit the base of the throat and pull the tongue down and out. Cut it as close as you can to its root. It's always good to get a little tongue!

BRAIN: For horror-movie fans, this should be an easy one. Take meat saw and carefully lift off bone baseball cap.

HEART: The heart, usually tucked high in the chest cavity, is connected to large blood vessels. When you cut it open, you'll see the chambers where romantic animal thoughts are thought to reside.

Camp Meat
What to Do with Them

For the quick roadside snack, camp meats sit high on the list. They always come through—well, almost always—intact, and make a nice pick-me-upper.

KIDNEYS: Broil or chop and add to a stew or dice and add to a gravy. It's good to fry as an accompaniment to a steak.

LIVER: This delicacy is reserved for special occasions, such as the completion of a successful shopping trip. Skin the meat and cut into long thin strips. Saute in a garlic or onion-flavored butter for 1 minute on each side and serve promptly.

TONGUE: Clean thoroughly with a stuff brush. Boil in a pot of water. Change water, add salt, pepper, trim excess and roots and simmer until tender. Let cool. Slice crosswise and serve on good dark bread with catsup, mustard, and horseradish handy.

BRAIN: Soak brain in cold water 1 hour. Trim off membrane and blood clots. Parboil 5 minutes in lightly salted water and with a tablespoon of vinegar. Drain and cut into cubes. Melt butter in skillet and when it bubbles, add brain. Brown butter, squeeze a lemon on top and serve immediately on toast.

HEART: Remove all membrane, clots, and fat. Wash well. Stuff with favorite dressing. Season. Roll in flour and brown in a heavy skillet. Bake in a covered dish at 350° for under 2 hours. Make gravy from drippings.

Roadside Cooking

In a familiar and friendly neighborhood, you can determine if you have the time to cook up a roadside snack. This can be done in several ways:

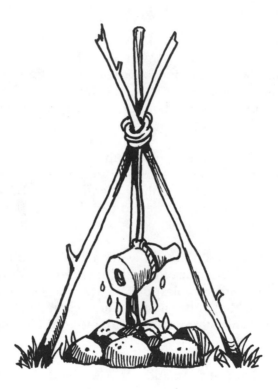

Or just lay a couple choice strips along the exhaust manifold.

In a less friendly spot, you'd best move your purchase to a more private area where a barbecue pit would work best:

Or put 10 lb. chunks on coals, cover with dirt, and cook for up to 10 hours.

Home Cooking

In your own castle, you can do much as you'd like. Many like to hang a skinned, gutted carcass in their basement, garage, or kitchen for a week or so while aging. It's not wise to throw hide or large bones in the yard as it attracts the attention of Miss Marple and her police radio.

Dutch Oven Cooking

Use this great item for everything. It's used to brown meat then sauteing the good stuff like onions and green peppers. Then adding your favorite combination of vegetables, wine, sugar, and oil and add meat again and roast in a pre-heated 350° oven for 2 to 2½ hours while basting with juices. This can cook anything.

• In a frying pan, you can cook anything too. With red meat, sear both sides, capturing the essential essences, lower heat to simmer, add one can of mushroom soup and cook until done.

• Never tell your dinner guests what they are eating until they are done!

• Never tell how you came upon the supply of game. Roll your eyes skyward, hands folded over your stomach and mumble about your classic confrontations with large dangerous animals, hint a dash of danger, yet concern about clean kills.

Buck's Butcher Shop

Large animals need special attention. Think of them as large machines; big, hot machines. To get the meat you want as good as it can be, there are several thoughts:

1. Cool the Meat!

If you've shopped in Wyoming during the early fall, it is important to take off the skin coveralls these critters wear. It's like you sitting at the beach with your Helly Hanson foul weather gear on. Skinning also tells you what meat you can use! All you need is a sharp knife. Buck normally starts where the chest stops and the belly starts with a small incision and cut like you'd open a coat, keeping the blade edge towards the skin. Cut and pull, cut and pull. When you get to places you can't cut and pull, cut it off—like the head, feet, etc. You're not legal so the extra time you spend carving an elk may just be enough time for a badge to walk up on you! Keep the meat covered and out of direct sunlight as you escape home.

2. Clean the Meat

Field dress Bambi as soon as possible. Their vital organs come in a Hefty Glad-like bag; carefully cut this loose. If it's already broken or you've drunk and you cut it, just get it all out as soon as possible, watching for valuable camp meats (see Camp Meats). Pull all of it out—then break the brisket or chest bone all the way to the throat and spread it with a stick for ventilation. Cut out the windpipe and esophagus too. Wash the meat and dry if possible.

3. Remove the Meat

Go home! You're not watched there. You can trim the damaged meat in the safety of your basement. Once near a sink, again wash the meat carefully and cut out the discolored and torn flesh.

4. Process the Meat

If you have a big critter like a moose, you'll have quartered the animal already. Buck always ages the meat of an old bull a week or two. The aging forms a crust which when shaved off reveals the finest in red aged meats. When you've got everything ready to go, the carcass will look like this picture, and each part has a name.

It's not necessary to know these names. They are part of the arcane language of overpaid meatcutters. It's really more important to know terms such as top, bottom, front, back, inside, outside, fur-side out, this and that (as in Give me some of that!).

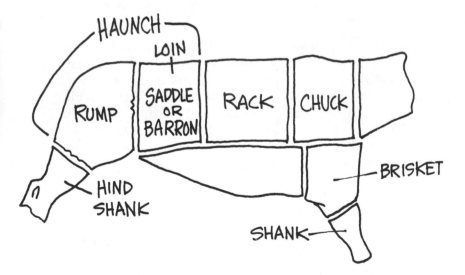

Rump will be called bum in Canada.

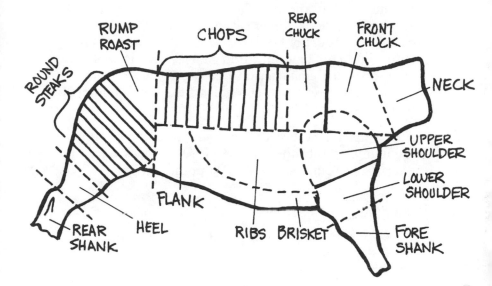

Now, start slicing like in the picture, working on a side at a time.

All cut up, the carcass has new supermarket names. When you start wrapping the meat, label the pieces accurately. Your freezer will read just like a Safeway meat counter and you'll be able to pick out the best cuts to go to the in-laws or neighbors (Buck likes to "shank" his!).

For those of you who are nervous about their first cutting, buy a bottle of Black or Yukon Jack, put the meat and knives on a good long table in the shed, turn on a good country station and have at it. On a small animal like antelope, just look it over carefully—you'll figure out the cuts. You made it out of the woods okay. The main thing is to take your time and don't have anyone look over your shoulder! Remember, one man's pork chop is another's rib eye. Last resort is to cut it all off the bones and make hamburger out of it.

Buck's first time was with two other mountain goats from Wyoming, and it took a quart of Yukon Jack and a full afternoon to cut and wrap a 700-pound moose.

SEVERAL SUGGESTIONS

Have water buckets handy for rinsing.
Knife sharpener.
Plenty of waxed freezer paper. Buck recommends poly-wrap first then freezer paper for large chunks.
Plenty of rags or paper towels.
Tape that will hold and not tear if wet.
Marking pen to identify cuts and year, and number of servings.

There are several advantages to doing your own. You get the cuts you want, with your own meat, can debone as needed to fit your freezer space, and do all this in the privacy of your own home. It's impossible to bring certain shoppers specials, particularly those with brands, to commercial shops without raising uncomfortable questions.

Everybody has an opinion as to preferred cuts. Now Buck doesn't cut like shown. He'll take the hind quarters and separate the muscle groups, and then only take steaks by cutting crosswise to fiber. He'll also bone out the chops, not forgetting the tenderloin or backstrap that runs along the backbone. Not too fond of roasts, he'll cut all roasts into stew meat and turn all the rest, including rib meat, into Bambiburger or sausage. So, it's up to you. You can't goof it up!

It's very easy to prepare small game for the cobblestone cafe. Skin the beast, clean thoroughly, and cut up according to recipe or size of your cooking utensil.

Birds are the easiest to get ready for the table. Take off feathers by plucking or, as a last resort, skinning, and cut up like a chicken.

The author, "Buck," here standing in front of his Alaska lake home, grew up among the Finlanders of Minnesota and has eaten many Firestone fillets! His dinner guests have included captains of industry, motion picture stars and other notables and many, many more less notables.